PAMPHLET

VOLUME 5

MINDFULNESS

BE PRESENT

Written by Jeremy Gleim

ISBN 978-1-960805-10-2

For information about special discounts available for bulk purchases, sales promotions, fund-raising, and educational needs, contact Mac and Trees Publishing at info@macandtreespublishing.com

1601 29TH Street, Suite 1292
Boulder, CO 80301
www.macandtreespublishing.com

To

Mac and Wyatt

~Don't lose sight of the present...your moments are everything!

BE PRESENT

What is Pamphlet Mindfulness?

"Pamphlet Mindfulness" is a series of small volumes which describe how specific topics (breathwork, kindness, patience, etc.) relate to and benefit a mindfulness practice. The purpose of these brief works is to present information in a quick and easy-to-absorb way, so that you...the reader...can ponder and implement these concepts in ways that are conducive to your life and being. These are not meant to be exhaustive dissertations on the subject matter; rather, they act as quick reference guides to help you achieve and maintain more peace, awareness, and happiness in your life.

For those who purchased the paperback copy of this book, there are a few blank pages at the end for notetaking. I encourage you to jot down thoughts, ideas, or anything that comes to mind during the reading of this.

What is Mindfulness?

Mindfulness can be understood as both a practice and a philosophy, but it is not considered a religion. Let's explore this distinction a bit with some definitions.

Practice: prac·tice (noun)

The actual application or use of an idea, belief, or method, as opposed to theories relating to it.

Mindfulness is often associated with meditation and is commonly referred to as a practice. It involves intentionally bringing one's attention to the present moment, and cultivating a non-judgmental awareness of thoughts, feelings, and sensations. Mindfulness practices can be found in various traditions, including Buddhism, where it is often used to develop insight and compassion. However, one of the most beautiful things about mindfulness is that it is not exclusive to any particular religious or spiritual tradition. Mindfulness, therefore, can be practiced by individuals from diverse backgrounds and cultures to aid their unique lifestyles.

Philosophy: phi·los·o·phy (noun)
The study of the fundamental nature of knowledge, reality, and existence, especially when considered as an academic discipline.

Mindfulness is rooted in certain philosophical concepts, particularly those found in Buddhist teachings. It emphasizes the importance of non-judgmental awareness, acceptance, and being fully present in the moment. Mindfulness philosophy encourages individuals to observe their thoughts and emotions without attachment or aversion, fostering a greater understanding of one's inner experiences and the nature of reality.

Religion: re·li·gion (noun)
The belief in and worship of a superhuman power or powers, especially a God or gods.

While mindfulness has its roots in Buddhism, it is not inherently a religious practice; however, it can be practiced within the framework of various religious traditions as a way to enhance and strengthen one's spiritual journey. Mindfulness has been secularized

Realize deeply that the present
moment is all you ever have.
Make the NOW the primary focus
of your life.
~Eckhart Tolle

and adopted in various contexts, including psychology, healthcare, education, and corporate settings, where its benefits for mental well-being and stress reduction are recognized.

In summary, mindfulness is primarily considered a practice and philosophy that can be applied in a secular or spiritual context, but it is not tied to any specific religion.

BEING PRESENT (PRESENCE)

It may seem silly to dedicate an entire volume of **Pamphlet Mindfulness** to the concept of being present, since mindfulness itself is all about the cultivation of present-moment awareness. But consider this for a moment; how often throughout your day do you split your focus between two, three, or any number of tasks?

- Talking on the phone while driving, cooking, working, etc.
- Scrolling social media while your child, parent, partner, friend, etc. is talking to you.
- Listening to a podcast while you're cooking dinner, talking to someone in the room, and passively watching TV.
- Thinking about work, school, life while you eat.

Don't worry, we're all guilty of these behaviors. It's hard not to be preoccupied with multiple things when the pace of modern life moves so fast. Life can spin at dizzying speeds, and it makes you feel like you won't be able to keep up unless you do fifty things at once. Is that really the best way to approach life though...only partially focused on everything? This volume is about bringing awareness to your daily life and behaviors, and how practicing present-moment awareness during your routine activities can actually strengthen your mindfulness practice in profound ways.

What is Presence?

Being present, or being in a state of presence, means you are fully attentive to what is happening in the present moment. For example, it could be a conversation you are having with someone, a task you're working on, or simply taking in the sights and sounds of your surroundings. When you operate in a state of presence, you are not preoccupied with regrets or anxieties, troubled about the past or the future, and you are not lost in daydreams or fantasies. Being present simply means focusing your attention on the thing right in front of you...in the current moment.

Presence and Mindfulness

Presence is the cornerstone of mindfulness. Being present in the moment is the foundation upon which all other aspects of mindfulness are built. It allows you to observe your thoughts and feelings as they arise, acknowledge them without getting carried away by them, and return to the present moment with a sense of non-reactive awareness.

While present-moment awareness and mindfulness practices can be particularly helpful during times of turmoil, emotional distress, and during meditation, it's essential to recognize that these practices are not limited to such situations. Mindfulness is most effective when it becomes an integral part of your daily life, extending beyond difficult moments and meditation sessions.

It takes consistent dedication and focus for mastery of any endeavor. We all learn at different paces and the journey towards expertise is individualized and multifaceted; however, the essential ingredient for everyone is repetition. Deliberate practice, continuous

If you are depressed, you are
living in the past, if you are
anxious, you are living in the
future, if you are at peace, you
are living in the present.

~Lao Tzu

improvement, and a growth mindset is what moves us towards deeper understandings and mastery of our undertakings. If we genuinely desire to cultivate greater mindfulness, incorporating it into every aspect of our daily lives through consistent repetition is a powerful approach. By integrating mindfulness into our daily routines and activities, we can create a culture of presence, self-awareness, and inner peace.

When we spread our focus simultaneously between multiple activities, it breeds chaos...leading to anxiety and stress. The human brain has limitations on how much it can handle at once, and trying to divide attention between several tasks can reduce overall productivity and increase feelings of overwhelm. As a result, the quality of your work may suffer, and you may find yourself making more mistakes or taking longer to complete tasks.

On the other hand, when you concentrate on one thing at a time, you can allocate your mental resources more effectively. This allows you to delve deeper into the task, achieve a state of flow, and produce higher-quality results. Additionally, focusing on a single task can reduce mental clutter and help you stay organized, leading to a more relaxed and efficient workflow.

Presence and Relationships

Think about the people in your life who you have the most interactions with. This could be a partner, significant other, parent, child, boss, colleague, or the grocery store clerk. Now, think about the way you interact with these people. Who amongst them gets your undivided attention during interactions? Do all of them? Do any of them? How does it make you feel when you have to compete for someone's attention?

Relationships suffer when communication suffers, and communication is the bedrock upon which relationships are built, so being present in your relationships is paramount to their success.

Realistically, it's not always possible to give everyone our undivided attention all the time, as our lives are filled with various responsibilities and obligations. However, it is essential to prioritize being present and attentive during meaningful and important interactions, especially with those we have close relationships with.

For Managers

Stop typing, reading emails, or tending to other tasks when your employees need to talk to you. Focus your attention on them, so they know you are listening and are actively engaged in what they are saying. This simple behavior will go a long way in building trust with your employees, and it will strengthen your role as a leader.

For Partners, Significant Others, and Friends

Turn the TV off, put your phone down (silence it if necessary), and give your full attention to the person you are conversing with. This will show them that they are important and deserving of your undivided attention. This will also allow you to engage deeper in the conversation and provide more meaningful dialogue, insight, empathy, and validation.

When someone feels that they must compete for our attention, it can lead to feelings of neglect, frustration, or even resentment. It may make them feel unimportant or undervalued, and this can negatively impact the quality of the relationship.

In healthy relationships, being present and giving genuine attention during interactions can strengthen the bond between individuals. It fosters a sense of connection, trust, and emotional intimacy.

To enhance relationships, it's important to practice mindfulness and be present during conversations and shared experiences. By doing so, you acknowledge

There are only two days in the
year that nothing can be done.
One is called yesterday and the
other is called tomorrow, so
today is the right day to love,
believe, do, and mostly live.

~Dalai Lama

the other person's importance and demonstrate that you value the relationship. Active listening, empathy, and giving uninterrupted time whenever possible, can significantly contribute to the success and well-being of your relationships.

Presence and Goals

Being in a state of presence can significantly help people achieve their goals by enhancing focus, productivity, and decision-making. When you are fully present in the moment, you bring your complete attention and awareness to the task at hand. This can lead to several benefits that contribute to goal achievement.

Death by Notification (DBN)

Those chimes and vibrations you receive indicating receipt of a digital notification are murdering your focus.

It's an interesting phenomenon, how we can hear and single out the notification sound associated with our phone and recognize even its faintest tone amongst a sea of other stimuli. It's because we've trained ourselves, just like Pavlov and his dogs, that the sound of a notification, whether it's a chime, vibration, or any other distinctive sound, can trigger a sense of anticipation and excitement in our brains. We have conditioned ourselves to perceive these notifications as potentially rewarding or important, leading to a constant "on alert" state where we are always subconsciously waiting for the next one.

The sound triggers a small release of dopamine, which makes us feel good...even before knowing what the notification itself is regarding. Since the sound triggers the release of dopamine, our body is constantly "listening" for it. This constant "listening" for notifications can significantly hinder our ability to stay focused and be present in the things we are working on. Each time a notification interrupts us, our attention is diverted from the task at hand to the incoming message, email, or social media update. This disrupts our flow of thought and it can take a considerable amount of time and mental effort to refocus on what we were doing.

Effectively managing interuptions can help reduce stress, improve focus, and maximize productivity. The perpetual state of anticipation and stress caused by constantly waiting for digital notifications can have adverse effects on our well-being. The repeated release of stress hormones, like cortisol, in response to notifications can lead to chronic stress and its associated negative consequences on our physical and mental health. Here's the good news; since we conditioned ourselves to respond to these inputs, we also have the power to recondition our responses to them.

The focus of this discussion has been on digital interuptions, because of their prevelance in modern society; however, you can employ the following strategies to mitigate other distractions as well.

Designate Focus Time
When you consciously decide to silence or mute notifications for a designated period, you send a clear signal to your brain that you are creating a distraction-free zone. This act of intentional disconnection gives your mind permission to shift away from the constant anticipation of notifications, which can lead to a release of stress.

By doing so, you allow yourself to enter a state of flow, where you can fully immerse yourself in the task at hand (presence). Flow is a state of deep concentration and engagement, and it can lead to increased productivity and a sense of accomplishment and fulfillment.

Starting with shorter time blocks, 20 or 30 minutes, is a practical and achievable approach. As you get more comfortable with this practice, you can gradually extend

The great science to live happily
is to live in the present.

~Pythagoras

the duration of your focused work sessions. Creating these interruption-free zones can also be empowering. It allows you to take control of your time and attention, rather than letting external factors dictate your focus. As a result, you may experience reduced stress and feel more in charge of your responsibilities.

For Managers and Supervisors

If your office serves as a proverbial revolving door, wherein you tend to have a continual barrage of employees asking questions, providing updates, etc., you can use this technique to your advantage. It's important to communicate to your team that you will be implementing some time-blocking techniques and part of that will include blocks of closed-door work sessions. These closed-door sessions will allow you to focus on something without the anticipation of someone entering your office.

By using time-blocking techniques and setting boundaries, you can strike a balance between being available for your team and having focused, uninterrupted work periods. This approach not only enhances your productivity but also helps you maintain a healthy work environment that respects everyone's time and priorities.

Batch Notifications

Instead of checking each notification as it arrives, batch them together at specific intervals during the day. This allows you to address them more efficiently and reduces the constant interruption. This can work for all types of notifications: email, social media, text messages, etc. Again, these are all strategies for creating a culture of presence, wherein you can enhance your ability to focus your attention on singular tasks.

The concept of batching notifications, or any task, is a way to create freedom in your daily life. If you place yourself at the mercy of your notifications, you are effectively allowing these things to hold your time hostage. By placing yourself in charge of when and how you respond to notifications and other things, you prevent them from dominating your schedule and dictating how you spend your time.

When you're constantly diverting focus to every notification as it arrives, you become highly reactive and lose the ability to focus on important tasks or achieve your goals efficiently. This can lead to a fragmented workday, reduced productivity, and increased stress as your attention is constantly bouncing from one thing to another.

Personal Life

Turn off your social media notifications and start dedicating specific time(s) throughout the day to engage with these platforms. With consistant mindful practice of this technique, you can condition yourself to prevent your socials from occupying massive amounts of your time, focus, and energy. This may also give you a newfound sense of control in your life.

Work Life

This may be very uncomfortable at first, but it will make massive improvements to your productivity if you start doing it. Dedicate specific time(s) to your email. If you are someone who always has their email open and tends to look at the sender/subject line of every email that comes in...in realtime...you are constantly diverting focus from the task you are working on.

Turn off email notifications and minimize your email window. As they continue to come in, your focus will not be hijacked by the notification and/or the subject matter. Allow them to stack up so you can finish other tasks. At a given time or interval, open the emails and hammer through as many as you can during the time block you have desiganted. Once the time for that block has expired, close your emails and work on something else.

Additionally, consider creating email filters or organizing your inbox to prioritize urgent messages and separate non-urgent

17

Be happy for this moment. This
moment is your life.

~Omar Khayyam

ones, making it easier to focus on critical communications during your dedicated email time

When implementing this strategy, it's essential to communicate your approach to your colleagues and supervisors to avoid any misunderstandings about your response times. You can set an auto-reply or create a status message indicating your designated email response hours and providing alternative contact methods for emergencies.

Over time, as you get used to this approach, you will likely notice significant improvements in your productivity and your ability to manage emails efficiently while maintaining focus on other tasks. It's a valuable technique for regaining control over your time and staying more present and productive in your daily work.

Presence and Growth

Practicing the ability to be present, even during the most ordinary tasks, can lead to a deeper connection with your surroundings and cultivate a greater appreciation for the simple things in life. Think about something you've done thousands of times...taking a shower, for instance. When was the last time you were in the shower, and you brought your full attention and awareness to the present moment and immersed yourself in the sensory experience of showering?

- The multiple distinct sounds of the water: when it flows out of the shower head, when it hits your skin, when it hits other surfaces in the shower.
- The temperature of the water on your skin.
- The way the soap smells.
- How the soap feels on your skin.
- How your fingers feel as they wash and move through your hair.
- The light in the bathroom. Is it natural or artificial?

Are there shadows?
- The sound of a fan or heater.

Have you ever engaged in this type of focused awareness during your shower? Next time you bathe, try focusing your thoughts and attention entirely on the act of showering. Allow your focus to meander from one sensation to another, there are so many stimuli to choose from. If your mind starts to wander to things outside the present moment, beyond the shower, bring yourself back to the shower by focusing on the water hitting your skin.

When you finish showering, acknowledge how you feel. Was it a pleasant experience? Was it peaceful? Was it meditative? Was it stressful or challenging? Mindfulness can be practiced in various situations and activities, not just during showering, but also while eating, walking, or engaging in any other routine task. Things like showering and eating have been performed thousands of times and require virtually no thought, so they are the perfect opportunities to work on your present-moment awareness. By consciously creating thoughts around these activities and observing the sensations you experience during them, you can train yourself to be more present and mindful in all aspects of life.

Becoming an observer of your thoughts, feelings, and emotions during menial tasks will help you observe these same things during more stressful or troubling experiences. It's a valuable practice that helps cultivate a more centered and peaceful state of mind, allowing you to savor the simple moments of life and find beauty in the present. Overall, integrating mindfulness into daily activities is a valuable practice that can have a profound

If you want to conquer the anxiety
of life, live in the moment, live
in the breath.

~Amit Ray

impact on your mental well-being and overall outlook on life. It helps you find moments of peace and connection in the simplest of tasks and equips you with a powerful tool for navigating the complexities of life with greater ease and resilience.

Cultivating Presence

Cultivating presence is a practice that involves training your mind to be fully engaged and aware in the present moment. It can be developed through regular practice and can lead to various benefits for your mental well-being and overall quality of life.

1. ***Mundane Tasks.*** Use your routine activities and tasks as a training ground for developing present-moment awareness. Focus on the sensations and sensory inputs you receive during these tasks and work on your ability to keep your attention on precisely what you are doing in the moment. Be patient with yourself and avoid self-criticism if your mind wanders. Gently guide your attention back to the task at hand and continue to cultivate this awareness throughout your routine activities.

   As you build this habit of mindfulness, you'll start to experience more of the unnoticed beauty and richness in your surroundings, leading to a deeper connection with the present moment and more appreciation for the simple things.

2. ***DBN Mitigation.*** Start using technology to your advantage, to better manage your digital notifications.

   a. Disable Non-Essential Notifications: Review the notifications you receive on your devices and identify which ones are essential and which ones are not. Turn off or disable notifications for non-essential apps or platforms. Prioritize notifications from important communication channels like work emails or urgent messages, and silence or mute notifications from social media, entertainment, or other non-essential apps.

b. Use "Do Not Disturb" and Focus Modes: Take advantage of the "Do Not Disturb" mode or similar focus modes available on your devices. Schedule specific periods or time blocks during the day when you want to focus on important tasks or simply need uninterrupted time. This setting will silence all notifications, allowing you to work without distractions.

c. Set Specific Notification Times: Rather than allowing notifications to interrupt your workflow as they come in, designate specific times during the day to check and respond to messages, emails, and other notifications. This way, you can maintain control over your attention and address notifications in a more organized and focused manner.

3. ***Implement Time Blocking.*** Start dedicating certain blocks of time to specific tasks (checking email and social media, meeting with employees, taking a digital break). During each time block, focus solely on the designated task and avoid distractions. Silence notifications and stay committed to the activity at hand...set boundaries.

Inform your colleagues, employees, team members, or partners about your time-blocking strategy. Let them know the specific times when you may be less available for immediate responses but assure them that you'll be more attentive during designated communication periods.

At the end of each day or week, review how well you adhered to your time blocks and evaluate your

To live in the present moment is a miracle. The miracle is not to walk on water. The miracle is to walk on the green earth in the present moment, to appreciate the peace and beauty that are available now.

~ Thich Nhat Hanh

productivity. Adjust your schedule as needed to optimize your workflow. It may take some time to get the blocks set up in the most efficient way, so while you're developing your structure stay flexible. It's important to remain flexible to accommodate unexpected tasks or urgent matters, provided they are truly urgent.

By incorporating these practices into your daily life, you can cultivate greater awareness and presence, which can help you achieve higher levels of focus, productivity, and mental well-being. Remember, mastery of any skill, including staying present in the moment, comes with practice and repetition. The more you engage in mindfulness and present-moment awareness exercises, the more adept you become at cultivating and sustaining your focus.

The Wrap!

Being present in everyday life is the foundation for building a stronger mindfulness practice. Mindfulness is about cultivating awareness and attention to the present moment without judgment. By consistently practicing presence in your daily activities, you naturally deepen your mindfulness skills.

Ultimately, being present in everyday life and nurturing your mindfulness practice are mutually reinforcing. As you continue to cultivate presence, you'll find that your mindfulness practice becomes more profound and fulfilling. The journey of being present is an ongoing and transformative process that enriches your life in countless ways, leading to a greater sense of connection, peace, and well-being.

Things to Ponder

- Practice Mindful Listening. Mindful listening, also known as active listening, is a practice of fully and attentively engaging in the act of listening to another person. It involves being present and fully focused on the speaker without distractions or interruptions. Mindful listening goes beyond just hearing words; it involves being receptive to the speaker's message, emotions, and intentions. This type of listening requires empathy, openness, and non-judgmental awareness.

  Mindful listening is a fundamental aspect of effective communication and building strong relationships. When you practice mindful listening, you create a safe and supportive space for others to express themselves openly and honestly. This type of active engagement fosters mutual respect and deeper connections with others, leading to more meaningful and fulfilling interactions.

- Using distinct sounds in your environment can be a helpful technique to anchor yourself in the present moment and enhance mindfulness. These sounds act as reminders to redirect your attention back to the present whenever your mind starts to wander.

  If you are outdoors, you can listen for the sound or call of a bird, the wind in the trees, or any other unique and distinctive sound that will remind you to be present. If you are indoors, it might be the sound of a fan, a ticking clock, or anything else that is easily identifiable to you.

  By using distinct sounds as anchors, you create opportunities to pause, center yourself, and reconnect with the present moment. This practice can be particularly useful during busy or stressful periods, helping you find moments of calm and mindfulness amidst the noise and distractions of daily life. With time and repetition, you'll find that you become more adept at using these sounds to cultivate mindfulness and stay grounded in the present.

NOTES

Made in the USA
Middletown, DE
16 August 2023

36815484R00018